TOP 10
NBA FINALS
MOST VALUABLE
PLAYERS

John Albert Torres

SPORTS TOP 10

Enslow Publishers, Inc.

40 Industrial Road   PO Box 38
Box 398   Aldershot
Berkeley Heights, NJ 07922   Hants GU12 6BP
USA   UK

http://www.enslow.com

Library of Congress Cataloging-in-Publication Data

Torres, John Albert.
    Top 10 NBA finals most valuable players / John Albert Torres.
       p. cm. — (Sports top 10)
    Includes bibliographical references (p. 46) and index.
    Summary: Profiles the lives and careers of Rick Barry, Larry Bird, Magic
Johnson, Michael Jordan, Hakeem Olajuwon, Willis Reed, Bill Russell, Isiah
Thomas, Bill Walton, and Jerry West.
    ISBN 0-7660-1276-X
    1. Basketball players—Rating of—Juvenile literature. 2. Basketball players—
Biography—Juvenile literature. 3. National Basketball Association. [1. Basketball
players.] I. Title. II. Title: Top ten NBA Finals most valuable players. III. Series.
GV884.A1 T69 2000
796.323'092'273—dc21
   [B]   99-044904

Printed in the United States of America

10 9 8 7 6 5 4 3 2 1

To Our Readers: All Internet addresses in this book were active and appropriate
when we went to press. Any comments or suggestions can be sent by e-mail to
Comments@enslow.com or to the address on the back cover.

Illustration Credits: Andrew D. Bernstein/NBA Photos, pp. 10, 13, 14, 17,
18, 21; Dick Raphael/NBA Photos, pp. 6, 9, 39, 41; Nathaniel S. Butler/NBA
Photos, pp. 22, 25, 34, 37; Walter Iooss, Jr./NBA Photos, pp. 31, 33; Wen
Roberts/NBA Photos, pp. 26, 29, 42, 45.

Cover Illustration: Andrew D. Bernstein/NBA Photos

Cover Description: Michael "Air" Jordan

Interior Design: Richard Stalzer

CONTENTS

INTRODUCTION

IT IS PROBABLY EVERY PLAYER'S DREAM to make the winning shot of a National Basketball Association (NBA) championship game. Children, growing up and playing basketball, pretend to hit the game winner as time winds down. But it rarely happens in the NBA.

Not many players are ever lucky enough to play on a team that is good enough to make it to the NBA Finals. Once players are in the finals, it takes a certain amount of luck, courage, and that certain will to win to lead the team to a basketball title. With millions of people watching, these players have to have nerves of steel. They cannot allow the pressure to get to them. They know that this, the NBA championship, is what they have spent an entire season, or an entire career, playing for.

But what makes a great NBA Finals Most Valuable Player?

This is not an easy question to answer. Sometimes a great NBA Finals MVP is a defensive player whose job it is to stop the opposing team's best player. He may be a fierce rebounder who will simply not allow the other team to take the ball and score. He may be a great team leader or a point guard who makes sure that the ball always goes to the open player. Sometimes he is just an inspiration to the rest of his teammates, maybe an injured player who gives his all in an effort to win. Many times, however, an NBA Finals MVP is the player who scores the most points. Often the guy with the incredible jump shot or the thunderous slam dunks ends up being the MVP.

Shooting guard Joe Dumars was named the Most Valuable Player of the 1989 Finals for the Detroit Pistons. His hometown in Louisiana honored him with a parade through town. Dumars knew what a special occasion that was. He was chosen the best player in a series filled with the greatest players. "A marvelous array of athletes has come through the NBA Finals," Dumars said. "I am very honored and very thankful to be merely one of them."[1]

But statistics alone cannot define what an NBA MVP is. If that were the case, players such as Karl Malone, Patrick Ewing, and Mitch Richmond would boast about being NBA Finals MVPs. Not everyone would agree on who the top ten finals MVPs are. But the ten players that we have chosen, at one time or another during a championship series, have been able to give their team that something extra, that inspiration, to help them become champions of the world. Players such as these have the most important statistic of all. They are winners.

CAREER PLAYOFF STATISTICS

Player	G	REB	AST	STL	BLK	PTS	APG	RPG	PPG
RICK BARRY*	74	418	340	106**	39**	1,833	4.6	5.6	24.8
LARRY BIRD	164	1,683	1,062	296	145	3,897	6.5	10.3	23.8
MAGIC JOHNSON	190	1,465	2,346	358	64	3,701	12.3	7.7	19.5
MICHAEL JORDAN	179	1,152	1,022	376	158	5,987	5.7	6.4	33.4
HAKEEM OLAJUWON	140	1,602	456	238	468	3,727	3.3	11.4	26.6
WILLIS REED	78	801	149	2**	0**	1,358	1.9	10.3	17.4
BILL RUSSELL	165	4,104	770	**	**	2,673	4.7	24.9	16.2
ISIAH THOMAS	111	524	987	234	38	2,261	8.9	4.7	20.4
BILL WALTON	49	444	145	32	83	528	3.0	9.1	10.8
JERRY WEST	153	855	970	0**	0**	4,457	6.3	5.6	29.1

G=Games   REB=Rebounds   AST=Assists
STL=Steals   BLK=Blocks   PTS=Points scored
APG=Assists per game   RPG=Rebounds per game   PPG=Points per game

*Does not include American Basketball Association (ABA) statistics.
**Statistics for some players are incomplete because steals and blocks were not recorded until the 1973–74 season.
All statistics are through the 1998–99 season.

RICK BARRY

Rick Barry shoots over fellow Hall of Famer Elvin Hayes of the Washington Bullets in the 1975 NBA Finals.

RICK BARRY'S CONFIDENCE HELPED make him one of the game's greatest players. Like most great players, Barry saved his best games for the championship series.

In 1975, Barry led the underdog Golden State Warriors to the NBA Finals against the heavily favored Washington Bullets, led by Elvin Hayes and Wes Unseld. Not many sportswriters or basketball experts gave the Warriors a chance to win the series, or even a game.

Golden State proved everyone wrong in Game 1, a 101–95 victory. For Game 2, the Bullets gave it everything they had to try to even the series. The Bullets jumped out to a thirteen-point lead, but Barry hit one jump shot after another. He took the team on his shoulders and scored an amazing 36 points, to bring his team back. The Warriors won, 92–91, and Washington seemed mentally defeated.

"We came back and won the ball game," Barry said, "and that was like the handwriting on the wall. They never recovered."[1]

Barry shook Washington again in Game 3 with 38 points, giving Golden State an insurmountable 3–0 lead. This time, Barry did a lot of his scoring from the foul line, after noticing that Washington was playing close attention to his jump shot. He would fake the jumper and then drive to the basket, drawing a foul. He made fourteen out of sixteen free throws.

The Warriors swept the NBA Finals in four games, which was a surprise. But it surprised no one when Barry was named the MVP of the series.

Rick Barry was born on March 28, 1944, in Elizabeth,

New Jersey. His father was his basketball coach at Roselle Park High School. The six-foot seven-inch Barry was named to the All-State team.

Rick Barry played college ball at the University of Miami. In college he was a scoring power, averaging 29.8 points per game in 77 college games. As a senior, Barry led all NCAA Division I players, averaging 37.4 points a game.

The San Francisco Warriors, later renamed the Golden State Warriors, chose Barry with their first pick of the 1965 Draft. He impressed right from the start by averaging 25.7 points a game. He made the All-Star team and was named Rookie of the Year.

In his second year, Barry showed what a clutch player he was. He led the NBA by averaging 35.6 points a game and helped lead the Warriors to the NBA Finals against the great Wilt Chamberlain and the Philadelphia 76ers.

Despite a badly sprained ankle, which required painkillers, Rick Barry saved his best games for the 1967 Finals. He accounted for almost all of the Warriors' offense. Unfortunately, that was all they had. Barry put up incredible numbers, including a 55-point performance in Game 3. He then scored 44 points in Game 6, but Philadelphia was too strong, and the Sixers won the series.

Barry played basketball for fourteen years. He was a twelve-time All-Star and the only player ever to lead the NCAA, the American Basketball Association (ABA), and the NBA in scoring. He was inducted into the Hall of Fame in 1987.

Rick Barry will always e remembered for his intense style and his will to win I was never the most popular player," Barry said. "I n r went out to make friends, I went out to win games.'

RICK BARRY

BORN: March 28, 1944, Elizabeth, New Jersey.

HIGH SCHOOL: Roselle Park High School, Roselle Park, New Jersey.

COLLEGE: University of Miami.

PRO: San Francisco Warriors, 1965–1967; Oakland Oaks (ABA), 1968–1969; Washington Capitols (ABA), 1969–1970; New York Nets (ABA), 1970–1972; Golden State Warriors, 1972–1978; Houston Rockets, 1978–1980.

RECORDS: Shares NBA Finals single-game record for most field goals made, 22; shares NBA single-game playoff record for most steals, 8; holds NBA All-Star Game single-game record for most steals, 8.

HONORS: Member of NBA championship team, 1975; NBA Finals MVP, 1975; NBA Rookie of the Year, 1966; All-NBA first team, 1966–1967, 1974–1976; NBA All-Star Game MVP, 1967; elected to Naismith Memorial Basketball Hall of Fame, 1986, NBA 50th Anniversary All-Time Team, 1996.

As a senior at the University of Miami, Barry led the nation in scoring with 37.4 points per game. He won two scoring titles as a pro, one in both the NBA and ABA.

Internet Address

http://www.nba.com/history/barry_bio.html

LARRY BIRD

Larry Bird shooting over Magic Johnson. The Boston Celtics captured three NBA championships in the 1980s, including one title against Johnson's Lakers.

LARRY BIRD

THE 1984 NBA FINALS WERE TIED, 2–2. The pressure was on and so was the heat. The temperature inside Boston Garden was ninety-seven degrees, because something was wrong with the cooling system. Everybody felt terrible in the heat, except Larry Bird of the Boston Celtics.

Bird decided not to get upset about the oppressive heat. He reminded his Celtics teammates that they should be used to playing in the heat. After all, he argued, they had all played outside during the summer months as kids. It should be nothing new, he told them.

Bird showed them what he meant. He torched the Los Angeles Lakers for a game-high 34 points. He made an incredible fifteen of twenty shots from the floor. The rest of the Celtics followed, and they blew out the Lakers, 121–103, to take the pivotal fifth game of the series. Bird was named the MVP of the series, helping Boston win its second championship in four seasons.

"I love to play in the heat," a smiling Bird said after the game. "I just run faster, creating my own wind."[1] In fact, the heat was nothing. Bird was used to finding ways to overcome adversity.

Larry Bird was born on December 7, 1956, in the small town of West Baden, Indiana. He was the fourth of six children born to Georgia and Joseph Bird. Larry became a star player at Springs Valley High School, in French Lick, Indiana.

Bird decided to attend Indiana University to play for legendary coach Bobby Knight. When he got to the college, however, Bird got homesick and decided to quit school.

Things got harder for Bird when his father killed himself in 1975. In 1976, Bird suffered a collapsed lung just as he decided to accept a basketball scholarship to Indiana State University. He overcame his difficulties, averaged 32.8 points per game, and led his team to a 25–2 record as a freshman. Bird was great again the next season, also averaging better than 30 points a game.

Bird was drafted by the Boston Celtics. As a rookie, he led a team that had won only twenty-nine games the previous year to a sixty-one victory season. He was voted the 1980 NBA Rookie of the Year.

In 1981, Bird led the Celtics to the NBA Finals. Boston faced off against the Houston Rockets, and star center Moses Malone. The Rockets led the first game late in the fourth quarter. That's when Larry Bird changed the game, and possibly the series. He put up a jump shot from the right side but immediately knew that the shot was off the mark. He rushed in to grab his own rebound. In midair Bird switched the ball from his right hand to his left and flipped up a twelve-foot shot that went right in. The crowd went wild, and the Celtics took the game, 98–95.

Boston's general manager, Red Auerbach, was ecstatic after the game. "It was the one best shot I've ever seen a player make," he said.[2] The Celtics won the championship in a six-game series.

Bird led the Celtics to five appearances in the NBA Finals and helped deliver three championships. He was named MVP of the 1984 and the 1986 Finals.

"The number one thing is desire, the ability to do the things you have to do to become a basketball player," Bird said. "I don't think you can teach anyone desire. I think it's a gift. I don't know why I have it, but I do."[3]

LARRY BIRD

BORN: December 7, 1956, West Baden, Indiana.

HIGH SCHOOL: Spring Valley High School, French Lick, Indiana.

COLLEGE: Indiana University; Northwood Institute; Indiana State University.

PRO: Boston Celtics, 1979–1992.

RECORDS: Holds career playoff record for most defensive rebounds, 1,323.

HONORS: Member of NBA championship teams, 1981, 1984, 1986; NBA Finals MVP, 1984, 1986; NBA Rookie of the Year, 1980; NBA regular season MVP, 1984–1986; All-NBA first team, 1980–1988; Long Distance Shootout winner, 1986–1988, NBA All-Star Game MVP, 1982; NBA 50th Anniversary All-Time Team, 1996; NBA Coach of the Year, 1998; elected to Naismith Memorial Basketball Hall of Fame, 1998.

The year before Bird was drafted, the Celtics won 29 games. In his first season, Boston suddenly became one of the best teams in the league, winning 61 games.

Internet Address

http://www.nba.com/history/bird_bio.html

MAGIC JOHNSON

Normally the point guard, Magic Johnson played center in Game 7 of the 1980 NBA Finals against the Philadelphia 76ers and scored 42 points.

TRYING TO PINPOINT ONE DEFINING MOMENT in the career of Lakers sensation Magic Johnson would be like trying to pinpoint one grain of sand on a beach. After all, Magic led the Lakers to five NBA championships in the 1980s and was named the MVP of three of those series.

Perhaps the series that opened America's eyes to his greatness was the 1980 NBA Finals against the powerful Philadelphia 76ers. The Lakers led the Sixers, three games to two, and seemed poised to win the championship.

Then, in Game 5, Lakers center Kareem Abdul-Jabbar sprained his ankle, and he was unable to play in the sixth game. The 76ers, with a powerful front line, including centers Darryl Dawkins and Caldwell Jones, could smell blood. Without Abdul-Jabbar, Philadelphia would have a good chance to win the series.

Lakers coach Paul Westhead asked Magic if he would like to try to play the center position. The rookie agreed. The plan was for Magic to use his speed and quickness, along with his strong low-post game to keep the Lakers in the game.

The plan worked to perfection. The 76ers seemed shocked and confused when they saw Magic take the center position at midcourt. Los Angeles scored the first seven points of the game, but Philadelphia regrouped and took a brief second-quarter lead. With five minutes left in the game, the Lakers held on to a 103–101 lead. Westhead called a timeout and told Magic to do his thing. Magic promptly used his quickness to draw foul after foul, scoring nine quick points as the Lakers finished off the Sixers. The game ended, 123–107. The series was over.

Magic finished the game with an incredible 42 points,

including 14 free throws, 15 rebounds, 7 assists, 3 steals, and a blocked shot. "Magic was outstanding, unreal," said Philadelphia guard Doug Collins. "I knew he was good but I never realized he was great."[1] Johnson was named the 1980 NBA Finals MVP.

Earvin Johnson was born on August 14, 1959, in Lansing, Michigan. Johnson loved playing schoolyard basketball. By practicing every day against bigger kids, he turned himself into a playground legend who could post low in the paint and handle the ball brilliantly.

He attended Everett High School and led his team to a state championship as a senior. After one game in which Johnson scored 36 points, had 16 rebounds, and passed for 16 assists, a sportswriter nicknamed him Magic.

He then accepted a basketball scholarship to Michigan State University. As a sophomore, Magic led his team to the NCAA Championship. He passed up his final two years of college and entered the NBA draft. He was the first player chosen in the draft, by the Los Angeles Lakers.

Magic went on to have a tremendous NBA career, winning five championships and many individual awards. He was named NBA Finals MVP after championships in 1980, 1982, and 1987.

On November 7, 1991, Magic announced to the world that he had contracted the HIV virus that causes AIDS. He has become an inspiration for people with the disease as he continues to fight it off and stay in good health.

In 1992, Magic made a brief comeback, playing in the All-Star Game and on the U.S. Olympic Dream Team. In 1996, he returned again for thirty-two games. Magic showed the world that having HIV is not an instant death sentence.

"This is going to tell tens of thousands of people with AIDS and HIV that they don't have to give up," he said. "They can just go on with their lives."[2]

MAGIC JOHNSON

BORN: August 14, 1959, East Lansing, Michigan.

HIGH SCHOOL: Everett High School, Lansing, Michigan.

COLLEGE: Michigan State University.

PRO: Los Angeles Lakers, 1979–1991, 1995–1996.

RECORDS: Holds career playoff record for most assists, 2,346; holds NBA Finals record for highest assists per game average, 14.0; shares single-game playoff record for most assists, 24; NBA career All-Star Game record for most assists, 127; NBA All-Star Game single-game record for most assists, 22.

HONORS: Member of NBA championship teams, 1980, 1982, 1985, 1987–1988; NBA Finals MVP, 1980, 1982, 1987; NBA regular season MVP, 1987, 1989–1990; IBM Award winner for all-around contribution to team, 1984; Citizenship Award, 1992, All-NBA first team, 1983–1991, NBA All-Star Game MVP, 1990, 1992; NBA 50th Anniversary All-Time Team, 1996.

Johnson has always been a winner. He led Everett High School to a state championship, Michigan State to a national championship, and the Lakers to five NBA titles.

Internet Address

http://www.nba.com/history/mjohnson_bio.html

MICHAEL JORDAN

With Jordan leading the way, the Chicago Bulls won six NBA titles in the 1990s. Jordan was named the Finals Most Valuable Player each time.

MICHAEL JORDAN

HE HAD DONE IT A HUNDRED TIMES BEFORE. Michael Jordan reached in and stole the ball from Jazz All-Star Karl Malone. Jordan raced downcourt, and dribbled to the top of the key. He faked a move left, just enough to free himself for a jump shot, and sank the winning basket, giving him and the rest of the Bulls their sixth NBA championship.

Jordan's incredible play in the 1998 playoffs earned him an unmatched sixth NBA Finals MVP Award. He is regarded by many as the best player ever to walk on a basketball court. And what makes Michael Jordan truly one of the best is his performance during the NBA Finals. He even scored 53 points during one finals game against the Phoenix Suns, on June 16, 1993.

Michael Jordan was born on February 17, 1963, in Brooklyn, New York. Soon after he was born, his parents, James and Deloris Jordan, moved the family to North Carolina.

Jordan went to Laney High School, making the varsity basketball team as a junior. At first, he was not one of the best players on his team, but he was the hardest worker.

Jordan became so good that he earned a basketball scholarship to the University of North Carolina. Jordan averaged 13.5 points as a freshman, and hit a last-second shot, to win the 1982 NCAA Championship. Jordan was named *The Sporting News* College Player of the Year after his sophomore and junior seasons, and then applied for the NBA draft.

Jordan was the third player chosen in the 1984 NBA Draft. Chicago had selected Jordan and he quickly turned the team around. Jordan averaged an incredible 28.2 points per game as a rookie and led the Bulls to their first playoff appearance in years. He was also named the NBA Rookie of the Year.

In 1991, the Bulls made it to the NBA Finals and squared off against the tough Los Angeles Lakers, who had won four titles in the 1980s. Jordan and the Bulls disposed of the Lakers in five games. Jordan stood at center court, holding the trophy high above his head and openly weeping. He was named series MVP. "I'm so happy for my family and this team and this franchise," he said. "It's something I've worked seven years for, and I thank God for the talent and the opportunity that I've had."[1]

The next season, Jordan established himself as an NBA Finals superstar, as the Bulls knocked off the Portland Trail Blazers. In Game 1, Jordan scored 35 points in the first half alone! He scored 46 points in Game 5, to give the Bulls a 3–2 series lead. Jordan had a strong fourth quarter in Game 6, helping give the Bulls their second championship in two years. Once again, Jordan was named the MVP of the Finals.

In 1993, Jordan and the Bulls won their third consecutive championship, and Jordan was once again the MVP. He had torched the Phoenix Suns for more than forty points in four of the six games in the series.

Jordan retired after the 1993 Finals to pursue a baseball career, but less than two seasons later, he was back, and the Bulls were ready to begin another quest for the championship. Jordan picked up where he had left off. In 1996, he led the Bulls to a title, defeating Seattle in six games. Jordan picked up his fourth NBA Finals MVP Award. It would not be his last. He won two more, as Chicago beat the Utah Jazz in consecutive years for two more championships, in 1997 and 1998.

Michael Jordan

BORN: February 17, 1963, Brooklyn, New York.

HIGH SCHOOL: Emsley A. Laney High School, Wilmington, North Carolina.

COLLEGE: University of North Carolina.

PRO: Chicago Bulls, 1984–1998, did not play during 1993–1994 season.

RECORDS: Holds NBA Finals single-series record for highest points per game, 41.0; holds career playoff record for most points scored, 5,987; holds career playoff record for highest points per game average, 33.4; holds NBA single-game playoff record for most points scored, 63; holds NBA career record for highest scoring average, 31.5.

HONORS: Member of NBA championship teams, 1991–1993, 1996–1998; NBA Finals MVP, 1991–1993, 1996–1998; NBA regular season MVP, 1988, 1991–1992, 1996, 1998; NBA Rookie of the Year, 1985; NBA Defensive Player of the Year, 1988; IBM Award, 1985, 1989; Slam-Dunk Champion, 1987–1988, All-NBA first team, 1987–1993, 1996–1998; NBA All-Defensive first team, 1988–1993, 1996–1998; NBA All-Star Game MVP, 1988, 1996, 1998; NBA 50th Anniversary All-Time team, 1996.

Jordan ended his career with a bang. He hit the game-winning jumper from the top of the key as time was winding down in Game 6 of the 1998 NBA Finals against Utah, giving the Bulls the title.

Internet Address

http://www.nba.com/playerfile/michael_jordan.html

HAKEEM OLAJUWON

In 1994, Hakeem Olajuwon became the first player in NBA history to be named the regular season MVP, Defensive Player of the Year, and Finals MVP.

HAKEEM OLAJUWON KNEW it was the only chance left to bring the 1994 NBA championship to the Houston Rockets. The big, sprawling center left his man, Patrick Ewing, alone in the post and raced out at New York Knicks shooting guard John Starks. Olajuwon jumped with his arms extended toward Starks, who had lined up for the game-winning three-point basket.

Starks was extremely hot. He had brought the Knicks back from 12 points down by scoring 16 of his 27 points in the fourth quarter. One more three-pointer in Game 6, and the Knicks would win the 1994 NBA Championship. Olajuwon gave everything he had to make it out to Starks in the nick of time. With two seconds left in the game, he reached out and tipped the ball as it left Starks's hand. The Houston Rockets won the game, 86–84, and took the wind out of New York's sails. Olajuwon led all scorers in the game with 30 points. He also had 10 rebounds.

Olajuwon's inspired play led Houston to a fairly easy victory in Game 7, for their first NBA Championship. As the final buzzer sounded, Olajuwon and his teammates hugged at midcourt. It was the ultimate moment in Olajuwon's awesome career. He was named the MVP of the series, becoming the first player ever to be named regular season MVP, Defensive Player of the Year, and Finals MVP.

All-Star center Hakeem Olajuwon had come a long way from his African hometown to center court where he hoisted a championship trophy over his head. "If you write a book, you can't write it any better," he said.[1]

Olajuwon was born on January 21, 1963, in Lagos,

Nigeria. When he was sixteen, Olajuwon was introduced to basketball. He loved the game and became very good at it. Many well-known colleges and universities were interested in offering him a basketball scholarship. It had always been Olajuwon's goal to become a scholar and study in an American school.

Olajuwon decided to attend the University of Houston. He helped lead the Houston Cougars to the NCAA Championship Game in both 1983 and 1984.

Olajuwon was then drafted in the first round of the 1984 Draft by the Houston Rockets. He had become very attached to the city, and was ecstatic to be able to continue his career there.

He made an immediate impact in the NBA. He averaged more than 20 points his very first season, establishing himself as one of the game's best centers. In fact, he was lucky and good enough to help his team make it to the NBA Finals in just his second year. The Rockets, however, were defeated by a very tough Celtics team in the 1986 Finals.

Olajuwon would be recognized as one of the top players in the game for many years. After winning the NBA title in 1994, he led the Rockets to the NBA Finals again a year later. In 1995, Houston's opponent would be the Orlando Magic, featuring Shaquille O'Neal and Anfernee "Penny" Hardaway.

Many experts predicted that the young Magic team would blow out the Rockets. Boy, were they wrong! Olajuwon dominated O'Neal, and Houston swept all four games from Orlando. Once again, Olajuwon was named Finals MVP.

"To win it the first time is a very unique feeling," Olajuwon said. "You don't know what it's going to be like until it happens. But to win it a second time is a different kind of thrill. You know the reward and that makes you want it even more."[2]

HAKEEM OLAJUWON

BORN: January 21, 1963, Lagos, Nigeria.

HIGH SCHOOL: Muslim Teachers College, Lagos, Nigeria.

COLLEGE: University of Houston.

PRO: Houston Rockets, 1984– .

RECORDS: Shares NBA Finals single-game record for most blocked shots, 8; shares single-game playoff record for most blocked shots, 10; holds NBA career record for most blocked shots, 3,459.

HONORS: Member of NBA championship teams, 1994–1995; NBA Finals MVP, 1994–1995; NBA regular season MVP, 1994; NBA Defensive Player of the Year, 1993–1994; IBM Award, 1993; All-NBA first team, 1987–1989, 1993–1994, 1997; NBA All-Defensive first team, 1987–1988, 1990, 1993–1994; NBA 50th Anniversary All-Time Team, 1996.

Olajuwon launches a shot over the outstretched arms of Magic center Shaquille O'Neal. In 1995, Houston beat Orlando to earn its second consecutive NBA Title.

Internet Address

http://www.nba.com/playerfile/hakeem_olajuwon.html

WILLIS REED

Although he was suffering from a severely injured leg, Willis Reed managed to start Game 7 of the 1970 NBA Finals. Using Reed's courage as inspiration, the Knicks captured the title.

WILLIS REED

THE LIGHTS GREW DARK, and the Madison Square Garden fans grew quiet with anticipation for Game 7 of the 1970 NBA Finals between the Knicks and the mighty Los Angeles Lakers. Rumors were circulating that the Knicks' star center, Willis Reed, would try to play despite a severely injured leg. If the fans were ever hoping for a miracle, they needed one now.

At 7:34 P.M., just before the opening tip, Reed, the team's captain, courageously limped out onto the court. The crowd went wild, and his teammates were filled with confidence. Reed was badly hurt, but he knew that he had to at least try.

"That was the championship, the one great moment we had all played for since 1969," Reed said. "I didn't want to look at myself in the mirror twenty years later and say that I wished I had tried to play."[1]

Somehow, Reed was able to outjump Lakers center Wilt Chamberlain for the opening tip. Reed even scored the game's first two points on a long jump shot from the top of the key. He then scored the second basket, a twenty-foot jumper. Reed did not score again in the game, but he did not have to. He inspired his team and demoralized the Lakers just by being out on the floor. The Knicks won the game, and their first championship, 113–99.

Willis Reed showed what heart and soul really were. In the first four games of the series, Reed scored 37, 29, 38, and 23 points, respectively. He also averaged 15 rebounds. Reed suffered an injury to his leg in the fifth game, which the Knicks managed to win. But without Reed for Game 6, New York was crushed, 135–113. He knew they could not survive without him in Game 7.

Many feel his dramatic entrance helped the Knicks win. "The scene is indelibly etched in my mind," said Knicks point guard Walt Frazier, "because if that did not happen, then I know we would not have won the game."[2]

Reed was born on June 25, 1942, in Hico, Louisiana. He loved to play basketball and became a star at West Side High School in Lillie, Louisiana. He won a basketball scholarship to Grambling University, where he became a force during his senior year when he averaged 26 points and a dominating 21.3 rebounds per game.

The Knicks selected Reed in the second round of the 1964 NBA Draft. He averaged 19.7 points and 14.7 rebounds per game, becoming the first Knicks player to win the NBA Rookie of the Year Award.

By the time the 1969 season arrived, the Knicks had established themselves as legitimate championship contenders. With incredible players, including Bill Bradley, Dave DeBusschere, Walt Frazier, and Willis Reed, the Knicks jumped out to a 14–1 record. They went on to win 60 games, and Reed was named the NBA's MVP. The Knicks, thanks to his inspiration, defeated the Lakers for their first NBA title. Reed was named MVP of the finals as well.

Three years later, the Knicks rolled to another finals appearance after posting a 57–25 record during the regular season. Once more, Reed inspired his teammates to victory over the Lakers. This time it took only five games, and Reed was once again named the MVP of the series.

After retiring from basketball as a player, Reed stayed involved as a head coach, assistant coach, and general manager for many years.

More than anything, Reed will always be remembered for the night he limped onto the court to inspire his teammates. "There isn't a day in my life that people don't remind me of that game," he said.[3]

WILLIS REED

BORN: June 25, 1942, Hico, Louisiana.

HIGH SCHOOL: West Side High School, Lillie, Louisiana.

COLLEGE: Grambling State University, Grambling, Louisiana.

PRO: New York Knicks, 1964–1974.

HONORS: Member of NBA championship teams, 1970, 1973; NBA Finals MVP, 1970, 1973; NBA regular season MVP, 1970; NBA Rookie of the Year, 1965; All-NBA first team, 1970; NBA All-Defensive first team, 1970; NBA All-Star Game, MVP, 1970; elected to Naismith Memorial Basketball Hall of Fame, 1981; NBA 50th Anniversary All-Time Team, 1996.

As a rookie in 1964, Reed averaged 19.7 points and 14.7 rebounds per game, becoming the first Knick to win the NBA Rookie of the Year Award.

Internet Address

http://www.nba.com/history/reed_bio.html

RUSSELL

THE NBA DID NOT START giving out Finals MVP awards
until 1969. But that does not mean that there were not any
Finals MVPs before that. In fact, the man who probably
would have won more than anybody else was Boston
Celtics legend Bill Russell. He won 11 NBA championships
as a player and player/coach for the Celtics, with his great
defense and rebounding.

Russell was also known for his seeming playoff domi-
nance of superstar scorer Wilt Chamberlain. The first time
the two players met in the championship was in the 1964
NBA Finals. Chamberlain was a powerful player, but Russell
quickly forced Chamberlain out of playing his normal game.
Near the end of a closely fought first game, Russell tricked
Chamberlain into taking a fadeaway jump shot. Russell
jumped up and swatted the ball away with authority.
Chamberlain's teammate Nate Thurmond grabbed the loose
ball and tried to shoot, but Russell blocked that as well. The
Celtics won their sixth title in a row.

William Felton Russell was born in Monroe, Louisiana,
on February 12, 1934. When he was a child, his family
moved to Oakland, California, where Russell became an
All-State basketball star. He enrolled at the University of
San Francisco and joined the college basketball team,
which won NCAA titles in 1955 and 1956. Russell delayed
turning professional because he wanted to be part of the
U.S. Olympic Basketball Team. Professional players were
not allowed to participate in Olympic sports back then.

Russell had experienced a lot of discrimination as a
child. It made him assertive when discussing the rights of

With Bill Russell blocking the way to the basket, opposing players had little room to shoot.

African Americans. He felt that it was very important to represent his country as an African American. He wanted to be a positive role model. Indeed, he led the Olympic team to a gold-medal victory in Melbourne, Australia.

Russell was drafted by the Boston Celtics in the first round of the 1956 Draft. He immediately provided the team with the type of dominating center they had needed for many years. The Celtics won the NBA Championship in Russell's first year. They finished in second place the next season, but then began a record string of eight consecutive NBA Championships.

Russell was such a dominating player that he was named the league's Most Valuable Player five times.

Another Celtics legend, point guard Bob Cousy, knew that there would have been no titles without the big, forceful center. "He [Bill Russell] was the ultimate team player," Cousy said. "Without him there would have been no dynasty, no Celtic mystique."[1]

In 1967, the Celtics chose Russell to be Red Auerbach's successor as head coach of the team. Russell became the first African-American head coach in NBA history. In fact, Russell was a player/coach from 1967 through 1969, winning two NBA titles in that time. He later coached the Seattle SuperSonics and Sacramento Kings.

Although he is not officially in basketball anymore, Russell is still visible at All-Star Games and charity events. He was elected to the Basketball Hall of Fame in 1974 and most recently was named one of the NBA's Top 50 Players of all time. Many people consider him to be one of the top ten.

When asked if he considered himself to be one of the best all-time players, Russell proved what a team player he really was. "I never concerned myself with that," he said. "My only concern was winning as many games as I could."[2]

BILL RUSSELL

BORN: February 12, 1934, Monroe, Louisiana.

HIGH SCHOOL: McClymonds High School, Oakland, California.

COLLEGE: University of San Francisco.

PRO: Boston Celtics, 1956–1969.

RECORDS: Holds NBA career playoff record for most rebounds, 4,104; holds NBA Finals record for highest rebounds-per-game average, 29.5; holds NBA Finals single-game record for most rebounds, 40.

HONORS: Member of NBA championship teams, 1957, 1959–1966, 1968–1969; NBA regular season MVP, 1958, 1961–1963, 1965; All-NBA first team, 1959, 1963, 1965; NBA All-Defensive first team, 1969; NBA All-Star Game MVP, 1963; NBA 25th Anniversary All-Time Team, 1970; NBA 35th Anniversary All-Time Team, 1980; NBA 50th Anniversary All-Time Team, 1996; elected to Naismith Memorial Hall of Fame, 1974.

Russell jumps high to challenge a shot. His archrival, Wilt Chamberlain, looks on.

Internet Address

http://www.nba.com/history/russell_bio.html

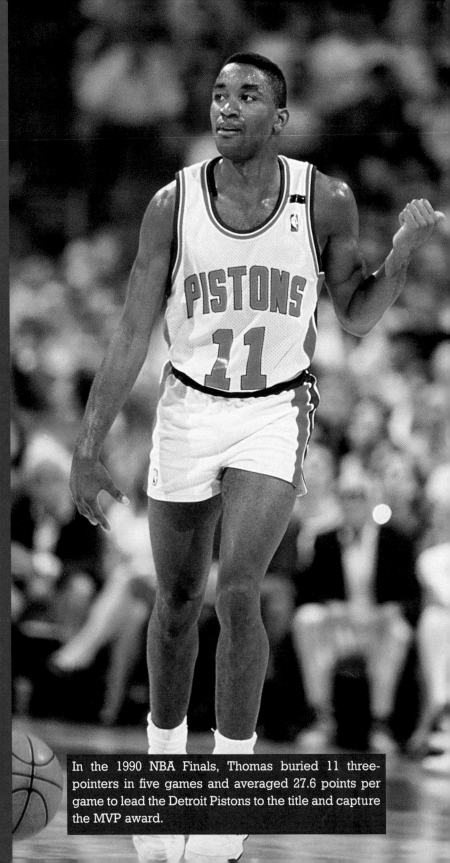

ISIAH THOMAS

In the 1990 NBA Finals, Thomas buried 11 three-pointers in five games and averaged 27.6 points per game to lead the Detroit Pistons to the title and capture the MVP award.

Isiah Thomas

THE PORTLAND TRAIL BLAZERS HAD PULLED AWAY, 94–89, taking a five-point lead late in the first game of the 1990 NBA Finals. With four minutes left, not many people were giving Isiah Thomas and the rest of the defending champion Detroit Pistons a chance to pull the game out. But Thomas had other things in mind.

It started on defense. Thomas stripped Portland's Terry Porter of the ball and then drew a foul. Thomas made both free throws and then made a long three-point jump shot, to even the score at 94. After another Portland turnover, Thomas drained an eighteen-foot jump shot, to give the Pistons the lead. After a missed shot by the Trail Blazers, Thomas brought the ball back upcourt and stopped in three-point range, looking to see what the defense would give him. Thinking Thomas would drive to the basket, Terry Porter took a few steps back. Instead, Thomas faked Porter, stepped back, and nailed another three-pointer, to seal the win.

Thomas finished with 33 points, including those ten in a row, to give the Pistons a 105–99 victory. Thomas credited his will to win for his inspiring performance. "It just kind of happened," he said. "This was a battle of wills, not a battle of skills."[1]

Thomas made 11 three-point shots in five games, and he averaged 27.6 points, as the Pistons cruised to a second consecutive NBA Championship. Naturally, Thomas was named the MVP of the series.

Isiah Thomas was born on April 30, 1961, in Chicago, Illinois. He grew up on the tough city streets but received a lot of inspiration from his mother. "The values that my mother instilled in us from an educational standpoint makes her my role model," Thomas said.[2] His mother, Mary Thomas, raised her nine children by herself.

Thomas starred in basketball from childhood. The shortest kid on the playground, he developed great quickness and leaping ability.

Thomas played high school basketball at St. Joseph's—in Westchester, Illinois—and was a huge hit. His point guard play propelled the team to the state title game when he was a junior, in 1978.

Many colleges recruited Thomas, but he chose to play for Head Coach Bobby Knight at Indiana University. Thomas impressed right from the start by averaging 14.6 points and 5.5 assists as a freshman.

As a sophomore, Thomas led the Indiana Hoosiers to the NCAA Championship. He then gave up his final two years at Indiana and decided to turn professional. He was the second player chosen in the 1981 Draft, by the Detroit Pistons. Thomas had always promised his mother that he would finish college, so he went back part-time and finished in six years.

Isiah Thomas went on to have a tremendous basketball career. He played in twelve All-Star Games, and led the Pistons to two world championships.

After retiring, Isiah Thomas was named to the NBA's 50th Anniversary All-Time Team. He also spent some time as a part owner and vice president of the Toronto Raptors basketball team. He continues to do a lot of charity work with poor youths. He even has paid for seventy-five students to go through college.

"As a person and a human being, if the only thing that I'm remembered for is playing a stupid game of basketball, then I haven't done a very good job in life," Thomas said. "Basketball is not everything to me."[3]

ISIAH THOMAS

BORN: April 30, 1961, Chicago, Illinois.

HIGH SCHOOL: St. Joseph's High School, Westchester, Illinois.

COLLEGE: Indiana University.

PRO: Detroit Pistons, 1981–1994.

RECORDS: Holds NBA Finals single-game record for most points in one quarter, 25; holds NBA All-Star Game career record for most steals, 31.

HONORS: Member of NBA championship teams, 1989–1990; NBA Finals MVP, 1990; All-NBA first team, 1984–1986; NBA All-Star Game MVP, 1984, 1986; NBA 50th Anniversary All-Time Team, 1996.

After leading the University of Indiana to an NCAA title as a sophomore, Isiah Thomas left college to play in the NBA. He later returned as a part-time student to earn his degree.

Internet Address

http://www.nba.com/history/thomas_bio.html

BILL WALTON

WITH ONE SECOND REMAINING in the sixth game of the 1977 NBA Finals, Philadelphia superstar George McGinnis put up a desperation jump shot. As soon as the wayward shot touched the rim, it was swatted away by Portland center Bill Walton.

Walton ripped the sweat-soaked jersey off his body and hurled it into the delirious crowd. The redheaded All-Star led the Trail Blazers to their first-ever NBA championship with a dominating series. That afternoon, Walton scored 20 points, grabbed 23 rebounds, blocked 8 shots, and passed for 7 assists.

Philadelphia's best player, Julius "Doctor J" Erving was dejected after the game, yet he paid Walton the ultimate compliment. "He's an inspiration!"[1]

William Theodore Walton III was born on November 5, 1952, in San Diego, California. He started playing basketball while he was in the fourth grade. A few years later, Walton became a basketball star at Helix High School.

At Helix, Walton became a dominating player. He was bigger and stronger than many other kids his age, but what set Walton apart was that he was a true student of the game. He tried to be the best fundamental player he could be. Walton led his team to the Interscholastic Federation High School Title two years in a row, winning forty-nine straight games.

Well-known college basketball coach Denny Crum was an assistant coach at UCLA to Head Coach John Wooden. Crum heard about Walton when Walton was only a sophomore in high school, so he went to see him play.

Crum was amazed at what he saw. He told Wooden that Bill Walton was the best high school player that he had ever

Determined to grab the rebound, Bill Walton charges toward the basket.

seen. Wooden did not believe Crum, at first, but he offered Walton a scholarship when he graduated. As a member of the UCLA freshman team, Walton led the youngsters to a 20-point thrashing of the varsity team.

Walton led the UCLA Bruins to two NCAA championships and a college-record eighty-eight consecutive wins. He was also a star in the classroom. Walton was named academic All-American, which meant that he was both a good student and a great athlete.

Walton was the first player chosen in the 1974 NBA Draft, by the Portland Trail Blazers. His first two seasons of pro ball were marked by nagging foot injuries. He finally enjoyed a relatively injury-free season in 1976–77 and led the Blazers to a title against the highly favored Philadelphia 76ers. Walton was chosen the MVP for the series.

The next season, all the pieces were in place for Portland to make another run at the title. Indeed, the Trail Blazers got off to a great start, and Walton was so good that he was named the league's MVP. But near the end of the season, he hurt his foot again. Portland was quickly eliminated from the playoffs without their star player. He would even miss the entire next season.

After Portland, Walton played for the San Diego and Los Angeles Clippers for five injury-plagued years, before taking a backup role with the Boston Celtics in 1986. That season he was voted the NBA's Sixth Man of the Year for his rebounding and defense. He was an integral player, helping the Celtics win the 1986 NBA championship.

Today, Walton remains active in basketball through clinics, camps, coaching, and television commentary.

"Bill Walton is the best player, best competitor, best person, I have ever coached," Blazers coach Jack Ramsey said after Bill had led Portland to the championship.[2]

BILL WALTON

BORN: November 5, 1952, La Mesa, California.

HIGH SCHOOL: Helix High School, La Mesa, California.

COLLEGE: UCLA.

PRO: Portland Trail Blazers, 1974–1979; San Diego Clippers, 1979–1984; Los Angeles Clippers, 1984–1985; Boston Celtics, 1985–1987.

RECORDS: Holds NBA Finals single-game record for most defensive rebounds, 20; shares NBA Finals single-game record for most blocked shots, 8.

HONORS: Member of NBA championship teams, 1977, 1986; NBA Finals MVP, 1977; NBA regular season MVP, 1978; NBA Sixth Man Award, 1986; All-NBA first team, 1978; NBA All-Defensive First Team, 1977–1978; elected to Naismith Memorial Basketball Hall of Fame, 1993; NBA 50th Anniversary All-Time Team, 1996.

At UCLA, Walton led the Bruins to two NCAA championships and a college-record 88 consecutive wins.

Internet Address

http://www.nba.com/history/walton_bio.html

JERRY WEST

Even though the Lakers lost to the Celtics in the NBA Finals in 1969, Jerry West was so dominant he was still named the Most Valuable Player.

JERRY WEST

HIS HAMSTRING MUSCLE WAS TORN, and Jerry West could hardly walk. He convinced the team doctor to shoot a painkilling medication into his leg so he could play. After all, it was the seventh game of the 1969 NBA Finals. West and his Los Angeles Lakers were tied with the Boston Celtics, three games apiece.

West limped onto the court and seemed to be breathing fire. He would not let the injury affect his play, or let it become an excuse. His eyes were fixed on the court, and his face was red with anticipation.

West hit the first shot of the game and never slowed down. But the Celtics, led by Bill Russell, took a seventeen-point lead early in the fourth quarter. Jerry West knew that if his Lakers had a chance to win, it would be up to him. He went to work at taking over the game. He quickly scored five consecutive points, cutting the lead to twelve. West saw opening after opening and kept driving to the basket, drawing fouls. The Celtics had no one that could stop him. Almost single-handedly, he brought the Lakers to within three points, 103–100.

But it would not be enough. Even though he scored 42 points, pulled down 13 rebounds, and passed for 12 assists, the Lakers lost the game, and the championship, 108–106. After the game, several Celtics players walked straight past their locker room to the Lakers locker room. Celtics great John Havlicek found Jerry West.

"Jerry, I love you," he said.[1] Then, Bill Russell took West's hand and held it for a long time without saying a word. The Celtics players were happy to win the championship, but they also felt bad for the great warrior Jerry West.

West was named the MVP of the series, after also scoring 53 and 41 points in two of the other games. It was the first time that a player from a losing team was named the MVP.

Years later, the loss still stung one of basketball's all-time greatest players. "I didn't think it was fair," West said. "That you could give so much and maybe play until there was nothing left in your body to give, and you couldn't win."[2]

Jerry West was born May 28, 1938, in Cheylan, West Virginia, a very small town. West was the fifth of six children but grew up very lonely in Cheylan. His father had to work many long hours. Jerry was close to his older brother, David, who died in the Korean War when Jerry was only twelve. West would go to his neighbors' house to use their hoop, and there he learned how to shoot from every possible angle.

The summer before high school, West grew six inches, and he made the high school basketball team. He eventually led his team to the 1956 state championship. West then went to West Virginia University and became a college basketball star.

West had a great NBA career and was known for his rugged style and smart play on the court. He was no stranger to championship play, as he made it to the finals nine times in his thirteen-season NBA career. He finally was part of a winning team in 1972, when the Lakers won a record thirty-three straight games and then beat the Knicks in five games, for the NBA crown.

After retiring, West coached the Lakers for three seasons before stepping into the front office as a general manager and team president. In 1979, he was elected to the Naismith Memorial Basketball Hall of Fame. Then he helped put together some of the great Lakers teams of the 1980s. The Lakers won five championships that decade.

West hated to lose. "He took a loss harder than anyone I've ever seen," said Lakers announcer Chick Hearn. "A loss just ripped his guts out."[3]

JERRY WEST

BORN: May 28, 1938, Cheylan, West Virginia.

HIGH SCHOOL: East Bank High School, East Bank, West Virginia.

COLLEGE: West Virginia University.

PRO: Los Angeles Lakers, 1960–1974.

RECORDS: Holds single-series playoff record for highest points-per-game average, 46.3; holds single-season record for most free throws made, 840.

HONORS: Member of NBA championship team, 1972; NBA Finals MVP, 1969 (for losing team); All-NBA first team, 1962–1967, 1970–1973; NBA All-Defensive first team, 1970–1973; NBA All-Star Game MVP, 1972; elected to Naismith Memorial Basketball Hall of Fame, 1979; NBA 35th Anniversary All-Time Team, 1980; NBA 50th Anniversary All-Time Team, 1996.

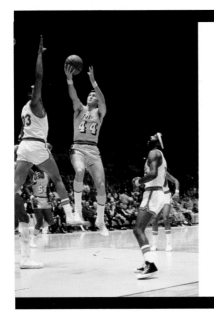

As the general manager and president of the Lakers, West helped form the great Lakers teams of the 1980s that won five championships.

Internet Address

http://www.nba.com/history/west_bio.html

CHAPTER NOTES

Introduction
1. Roland Lazenby, *The NBA Finals: A Fifty-Year Celebration* (Lincolnwood, Ill.: Masters Press, 1996), p. 1.

Rick Barry
1. Roland Lazenby, *The NBA Finals: A Fifty-Year Celebration* (Lincolnwood, Ill.: Masters Press, 1996), p. 176.
2. "Basketball Has Been Barry, Barry Good to Them," Associated Press, November 18, 1995.

Larry Bird
1. Roland Lazenby, *The NBA Finals: A Fifty-Year Celebration* (Lincolnwood, Ill.: Masters Press, 1996), p. 234.
2. Ibid., p. 215.
3. Ibid., p. 231.

Magic Johnson
1. Roland Lazenby, *The NBA Finals: A Fifty-Year Celebration* (Lincolnwood, Ill.: Masters Press, 1996), p. 210.
2. Associated Press, October 6, 1992, as appeared in the *San Jose Mercury News*.

Michael Jordan
1. Roland Lazenby, *The NBA Finals: A Fifty-Year Celebration* (Lincolnwood, Ill.: Masters Press, 1996), p. 290.

Hakeem Olajuwon
1. John Albert Torres, *Hakeem Olajuwon: Star Center* (Springfield, N.J.: Enslow Publishers, Inc., 1997), p. 15.
2. Roland Lazenby, *The NBA Finals: A Fifty-Year Celebration* (Lincolnwood, Ill.: Masters Press, 1996), p. 314.

Willis Reed
1. Roland Lazenby, *The NBA Finals: A Fifty-Year Celebration* (Lincolnwood, Ill.: Masters Press, 1996), p. 149.
2. Ibid., p. 150.
3. "NBA Legends: Willis Reed," *NBA History*, 1998, <http://www.nba.com/history/reed_bio.html> (April 16, 1999).

Bill Russell

1. Roland Lazenby, *The NBA Finals: A Fifty-Year Celebration* (Lincolnwood, Ill.: Masters Press, 1996), p. 80.

2. "Bill Russell at 1997 NBA All-Star Weekend," *ASAP FastScripts*, February 7, 1997, <http://www.asapsports.com/basketball/1997allstar/020797BR.html> (April 16, 1999).

Isiah Thomas

1. Roland Lazenby, *The NBA Finals: A Fifty-Year Celebration* (Lincolnwood, Ill.: Masters Press, 1996), p. 274.

2. "NBA Legend Isiah Thomas," *CBS Sportsline Chat*, February 2, 1999, <http://cbs.sportsline.com/u/chat/isiah020299.htm> (April 16, 1999).

3. "NBA Legends: Isiah Thomas," *NBA History*, 1998, <http://www.nba.com/history/thomas_bio.html> (April 16, 1999).

Bill Walton

1. Roland Lazenby, *The NBA Finals: A Fifty-Year Celebration* (Lincolnwood, Ill.: Masters Press, 1996), p. 189.

2. Ibid., p. 194.

Jerry West

1. "Jerry West," *NBA History*, 1998, <http://www.nba.com/history/west_bio.html> August 30, 1999. As appeared in Scott Ostler, "Pursuing Perfection: From Basketball to Golf, Hall of Famer Jerry West Is Driven to Be the Best," *National Sports Daily*, February 5, 1990.

2. Roland Lazenby, *The NBA Finals: A Fifty-Year Celebration* (Lincolnwood, Ill.: Masters Press, 1996), p. 139.

3. "Jerry West," *NBA History*.

Index